CREED
CHILDREN'S LEADER GUIDE

Creed
WHAT CHRISTIANS BELIEVE AND WHY

Creed
978-1-5018-1371-9 *Book*
978-1-5018-1372-6 *eBook*
978-1-5018-1373-3 *Large Print*

Creed: Leader Guide
978-1-5018-1374-0 *Book*
978-1-5018-1375-7 *eBook*

Creed: DVD
978-1-5018-1376-4

Creed: Children's Leader Guide
978-1-5018-1370-2

Creed: Youth Study Book
978-1-5018-1383-2 *Book*
978-1-5018-1384-9 *eBook*

Creed: Leader Kit (One of each)
978-1-5018-2483-8

Adam Hamilton

CREED

What Christians Believe and Why

Children's Leader Guide
by Sally Hoelscher

Abingdon Press / Nashville

CREED:
WHAT CHRISTIANS BELIEVE AND WHY
CHILDREN'S LEADER GUIDE

This book is printed on elemental chlorine-free paper.

ISBN 978-1-5018-1370-2

16 17 18 19 20 21 22 23 24 25 — 10 9 8 7 6 5 4 3 2 1
MANUFACTURED IN THE UNITED STATES OF AMERICA

Contents

To the Leader

This Children's Leader Guide is designed for use with Adam Hamilton's book *Creed: What Christians Believe and Why*. This guide includes six lessons that take a look at the Apostles' Creed. Children will explore what Christians believe as they study the Apostles' Creed. This study contains six lessons and may be used as a Lenten study, but is designed to be usable at any time during the year.

In addition to the book, the program includes a DVD, Leader Guide, Youth Study Book, and this Children's Leader Guide.

The lessons in this guide, designed for children in kindergarten through the sixth grade, are presented in a large-group/small-group format. Children begin with time spent at activity centers, followed by time together as a large group. Children end the lesson in small groups determined by age. Each lesson plan contains the following sections:

Focus for the Teacher

The information in this section will provide you with background information about the week's lesson. Use this section for your own study as you prepare.

Explore Interest Groups

You'll find ideas for a variety of activity centers in this section. These activities will prepare the children to hear the Bible story. Allow the children to choose one or more of the activities that interest them. Occasionally there will be an activity that is recommended for all children, usually because it relates directly to a later activity. When this is the case, it will be noted.

Large Group

The children will come together as a large group to hear the story for the week. This section begins with a transition activity followed by the story and a Bible verse activity. A worship time concludes the large-group time.

Small Groups

Children are divided into age-level groups for small-group time. Depending on the size of your class, you may need to have more than one group for each age level. It is recommended that each small group contain no more than ten children.

Younger Children
The activities in this section are designed for children in grades K–2.

Older Children
The activities in this section are designed for children in grades 3–6.

Reproducible Pages

At the end of each lesson are reproducible pages, to be photocopied and handed out for all the children to use during that lesson's activities.

Schedule

Many churches have weeknight programs that include an evening meal, an intergenerational gathering time, and classes for children, youth, and adults. The following schedule illustrates one way to organize a weeknight program.

5:30 p.m.	Meal
6:00 p.m.	Intergenerational gathering introducing weekly themes and places for the lesson. This time may include presentations, skits, music, and opening or closing prayers.
6:15 p.m.–8:15 p.m.	Classes for children, youth, and adults.

Churches may want to do this study as a Sunday school program. This setting would be similar to the weeknight setting. The following schedule takes into account a shorter class time, which is the norm for Sunday morning programs.

10 minutes	Intergenerational gathering
45 minutes	Classes for children, youth, and adults

Choose a schedule that works best for your congregation and its existing Christian education programs.

Blessings to you and the children as you explore the Apostles' Creed and the basics of Christian faith!

1. God

Objectives

The children will:

• learn about the Apostles' Creed.

• discover that Christians believe in God who created the world.

• explore why belief in God matters in their lives.

Theme

Christians believe in God.

Bible Verse

Heaven is declaring God's glory;
   the sky is proclaiming his handiwork.
                                    (Psalm 19:1)

Focus for the Teacher

What do Christians believe? The answer to that question will certainly differ when looking at various denominations of the Christian faith. Even within a denomination, individual Christians hold a variety of beliefs on many topics. Yet on certain fundamental things, Christians agree. Throughout history, groups of Christians have attempted to put their core beliefs in writing. These attempts have resulted in a number of creeds and affirmations of faith. This study will use the Apostles' Creed to examine what Christians believe and why these particular beliefs are important.

Each of the six lessons in this study will examine a section of the Apostles' Creed. The emphasis of the lessons will be on looking at what Christians believe and how those beliefs shape our actions. Each week children will have an opportunity to say words of the Apostles' Creed, adding sections of the creed as they are discussed. Although children may not understand all the wording used in the Apostles' Creed (nor do all adults, for that matter), they will become familiar with it and recognize the words when they hear the words in worship.

> Christians believe in a God who created the world.

The study begins, as does the creed, with God. Christians believe in God. Specifically, Christians believe in a God who created the world and remains engaged with the creation, including us. The Apostles' Creed uses the term "God, the Father." "Father" was the term Jesus used to address God. It is a term signifying a relationship between God and humans. God did not create the world, set it in motion, and then sit back and watch what happened; God remains interested in the creation, including human beings. People are a small part of the vast expanse of God's creation. Yet God desires to be in relationship with us.

Why does believing in God matter? How does such a belief shape our lives? Believing in a God who cares about us means we are never alone. God is always with us. This is a reason to praise God. Faith in God leads to an attitude of gratitude for the creator and all of creation.

Explore Interest Groups

Be sure that adult leaders are waiting when the first child arrives. Greet and welcome the children. Get the children involved in an activity that interests them and introduces the theme for the day's activities.

Word Web

- Show children the diagram you have drawn.

- **Say:** This kind of funny-looking diagram is called a word web. Word webs can be helpful to explore the meaning of words. You can see that the word *believe* is in the center of our word web. What words does *believe* remind you of?

- Write one of the words the children come up with in each of the six ovals connected to the word *believe*.

- Take a look at the new words one at a time.

- For each new word, **Ask:** What words come to mind when you think of this word?

- Write the words the children come up with for each word in the outermost ovals.

- Invite the children to spend a few moments looking at your completed word web.

- **Ask:** What does it mean to say, "I believe" something? (to think something is true, to hope for something)

- **Say:** For the next six weeks we are going to be talking about what Christians believe.

Nature Speaks

- Invite children to look through the nature pictures you have provided.

- Encourage each child to choose one picture they like and glue it on a piece of paper, cutting it to fit as needed.

- **Ask:** What do all these pictures have in common? (They all show parts of nature.) Who created all the things shown in your pictures? (God.)

- **Say:** God created the world and everything in it. There are several verses in the Bible that talk about parts of God's creation praising God. Of course, the things shown in your pictures can't speak. They can't praise God the way you and I can.

- **Ask:** How does nature praise God without words?

- Allow children an opportunity to share their thoughts and ideas.

- **Say:** Right now you are going to use your imaginations to pretend that your pictures can speak. Imagine what words would be used by the things in your picture to praise God.

Prepare

✓ Cut a large piece of mural paper. In the center of the paper, draw an oval and write the word *believe* inside the oval. Draw six lines radiating out from the oval and draw an oval at the end of each line. Draw two lines from each of the new ovals and draw an oval at the end of each line.

✓ Display the mural paper where the children will be able to see it.

✓ Provide markers.

✓ Provide copies of **Reproducible 1a: Speech Bubbles**.

✓ Supply old magazines, paper, scissors, glue sticks, and pencils.

✓ Look through the magazines and tear out pictures of nature and nature scenes, such as mountains, trees, waterfalls, and sunsets.

✓ Option: If you have church members who take nature photographs, invite them to share copies of photographs for the children to use in this activity.

- Invite children to cut out one or more speech bubbles.
- Have children write words praising God on each speech bubble.
- Let the children glue the speech bubbles to their pictures.
- Encourage children to share their pictures with one another.
- Create a "Nature Speaks Gallery" by displaying the pictures in your classroom.

Prepare

✓ Provide a CD player and a CD of upbeat music.

✓ Set up a circle of chairs, facing the chairs to the outside of the circle and using one less chair than the number of children playing.

Musical Creation

- Have the children form a circle around the chairs.
- Start playing music and have the children begin walking around the circle.
- **Say:** When the music stops, find a chair and sit down.
- Stop the music and have the children find seats.
- **Say:** You are not out of the game if you are left standing. Instead, you will tell us something God created.
- Invite the child who is standing to name something God created.
- Continue playing the game, removing an additional chair each round before starting the music. As the game continues, encourage children to share parts of God's creation that have not been previously named.

Prepare

✓ Provide recyclable materials (such as plastic bottles, plastic containers of various sizes, lids, cardboard, and newspaper), craft sticks, chenille stems, construction paper, scissors, tape, and glue.

✓ Spread the recyclable and craft materials out on a table.

Creation Station

- Invite children to create something out of the available materials.
- Encourage children to use their imaginations.
- If a child creates something and doesn't like it, encourage him or her to take the item apart and make something else.
- **Say:** We are created in God's image. That means we resemble God. We can be creators like God is a creator.

Large Group

Bring all the children together to experience the Bible story. Use a bell to alert the children to the large-group time.

Created to Praise

- **Say:** Our God created a wonderful world. If you were a coyote, you might thank God for creating the world by howling.
- Encourage children to give their best coyote howl.
- **Say:** If you were a penguin, you might thank God by proudly waddling around in your black and white suit.
- Encourage children to waddle like penguins.
- **Say:** If you were a rooster, you might give a fine "cock-a-doodle-doo" to say, "Hey, thanks, God!"
- Encourage children to say "Cock-a-doodle-doo!"
- **Say:** Since we are people, let's clap our hands three times and stomp our feet three times to thank God for creating us.

Christians Believe in God

- **Say:** For the next six weeks we will be talking about what Christians believe.
- **Ask:** What's a Christian? (a follower of Jesus)
- Recruit six volunteers to read today's story.
- **Say:** As Christians we believe many different things. Some of them aren't very important. For example, I may believe that blue is the best color. You may believe differently. But there are certain important things that Christians agree on. Those are the beliefs we will be talking about.
- Give each volunteer a copy of **Reproducible 1b: Christians Believe in God**, and assign each reader a part.
- Have the readers stand in front of the class to read the story. Encourage children to speak loudly.
- Thank your volunteers for sharing today's story.

Prepare
✓ Provide copies of **Reproducible 1b: Christians Believe in God**.

Prepare

✓ Write the week's Bible verse on a markerboard or a piece of mural paper and place it where it can easily be seen. (Heaven is declaring God's glory; the sky is proclaiming his handiwork. [Psalm 19:1])

Prepare

✓ Write the first part of the Apostles' Creed on a piece of posterboard:

I believe in God, the Father Almighty, creator of heaven and earth.

✓ Display the poster where the children will be able to read it. Leave the poster up for the duration of the study.

Bible Verse in Two Parts

- **Say:** Our Bible verse for today is from the Book of Psalms.

- **Ask:** Is Psalms in the Old Testament or the New Testament? (Old Testament.)

- Show the children the Bible verse. Encourage them to read the verse with you.

- **Ask:** Who created the heaven and the sky? (God.)

- **Say:** Many people feel close to God when they are in nature. When we are surrounded by the beauty of God's creation, it can help us feel gratitude toward God for making such an amazing world.

- Divide the children into four groups.

- **Say:** We are going to say our Bible verse several more times. I will point to a group and hold up one finger. That group will say the first part of the verse, "Heaven is declaring God's glory." Then I will point to another group and hold up two fingers. That group will say the second part of the verse, "the sky is proclaiming his handiwork."

- Say the Bible verse several times, pointing to different groups.

I Believe in God

- **Say:** The first part of the Apostles' Creed says we believe in God.

- **Ask:** Why do you think belief in God is the first thing in the creed?

- **Say:** The Bible teaches us we are to put God first. Jesus taught that the greatest commandment is to love the Lord your God with all your heart, all your being, and all your mind. The Ten Commandments tell us we are to worship only God. It is appropriate that God is first in the Apostles' Creed.

- Show the children the poster you have made.

- **Say:** I have written the first part of the Apostles' Creed on this poster.

- **Ask:** Have you heard or said the Apostles' Creed before? When have you heard it? (Some churches use the creed in worship.)

- **Say:** Each week while we are studying what Christians believe, we are going to use the Apostles' Creed during our large-group time just before you go to your small groups. Today I will ask you, "What do you believe?" and you will respond with the part of the creed shown on our poster. Each week we will add another section of the creed.

- **Ask:** What do you believe?

- Encourage children to respond: I believe in God, the Father Almighty, creator of heaven and earth.

- Dismiss children to their small groups.

Small Groups

Divide the children into small groups. You may organize the groups around age levels or around readers and nonreaders. Keep the groups small, with a maximum of ten children in each group. You may need to have more than one group of each age level.

Young Children

- **Say:** As Christians, we believe in God and we believe God created the world.

- **Say:** Think of your favorite thing God created that makes you want to say, "Thanks, God, for creating that!"

- Allow children an opportunity to respond.

- **Say:** God created so many amazing things. God cares about creation, including us. God loves us and wants to be connected to us.

- **Ask:** How do we talk to God? (prayer) How do we find out what God wants us to do? (prayer, reading the Bible, talking to other people about God, going to church)

- Give each child a piece of paper.

- Have each child write the word *God* in the center of the paper.

- **Say:** God will never stop loving us and never leave us. God never forgets about us. Sometimes we get busy, though, and we forget about God. We have to work at staying connected to God. Some people feel connected to God when they pray or when they are in worship. Other people feel connected to God when they are in the mountains or beside a lake. Some people feel connected to God when they are with someone they love.

- Invite each child to draw several lines extending from the word *God* outward.

- **Say:** At the end of each line, draw a picture of something or someone that helps you feel connected to God.

- Invite children to share their drawings with one another.

- **Say:** Let's connect with God right now by praying.

- **Pray:** God, thank you for creating this amazing world and creating us. Thank you for loving us with a love that will never end. We believe in you and love you. Amen.

Prepare
✓ Provide paper and crayons.

Prepare

✓ Find pictures of space in books or on the Internet. NASA has a lot of images from the Hubble telescope on their website (http://www.nasa.gov/mission_pages/hubble/multimedia/index.html).

✓ Provide paper and pencils.

Older Children

- **Say:** As Christians, we believe in God and we believe God created the world.

- **Ask:** How big is the world?

- Show the children the pictures of space.

- **Say:** These are some pictures that have been taken of the world beyond our planet. Scientists are continuing to explore and discover more about God's amazing world.

- **Ask:** How do you feel when you look at these pictures? How do these pictures make you feel about God?

- **Say:** God created many wonderful things in this world, including us. Even though we are only a part of God's creation, God loves us and wants to be connected to us.

- **Ask:** How does it make you feel to know that even though you are only a part of God's creation, God loves you and will never stop loving you?

- Allow children an opportunity to respond.

- **Say:** When we consider all the things God created and then know that God loves us, it is appropriate to feel gratitude.

- **Ask:** What does it mean to be grateful? (to be thankful, to give thanks)

- Give each child a piece of paper and a pencil.

- Invite each child to write a thank-you letter to God.

- **Say:** In your letter, tell God what it means to you to be chosen among all of God's creation to be loved by God.

- Let children know that their letters are between them and God and they will not be asked to share them.

- Allow children time to write. Have the children fold their letters and hold them while you pray.

- **Pray:** God, thank you for creating this amazing world that includes us. Thank you for your never-ending love for us. Help us to remember to show gratitude for all you have done. Amen.

Speech Bubbles

Christians Believe in God

Friend 1: Well, here we are at church.

Friend 2: Time to talk about church stuff.

Friend 3: So what are we talking about today?

Friend 4: Something called the Apostles' Creed.

Friend 5: What's the Apostles' Creed?

Friend 6: Well, an apostle is a follower of Jesus.

Friend 3: Also known as a Christian, right?

Friend 2: Right. And a creed is a statement of beliefs.

Friend 4: So the Apostles' Creed tells us what Christians believe.

Friend 5: Cool! Since we are Christians, we should know what we believe.

Friend 6: Exactly!

Friend 1: So what do Christians believe?

Friend 4: The Apostles' Creed begins, "I believe in God, the Father Almighty, creator of heaven and earth."

Friend 6: I believe in God. That seems important.

Friend 3: I know the Bible uses many different names for God. Why does the creed talk about God as our Father?

Friend 2: *Father* is the name Jesus used when he prayed to God.

Friend 1: Addressing God as Father shows we are in relationship with God.

Friend 5: God loves us and will never stop loving us.

Friend 3: What was the rest of that…creator of heaven and earth?

Friend 6: Yes, God created the world and everything in it.

Friend 2: God created mountains, seas…

Friend 1: rocks, trees, planets, stars…

Friend 4: animals, and people. God created it all!

Friend 2: What else do Christians believe?

Friend 5: Come back next week to find out!

2. Jesus Christ

Objectives

The children will:

- learn about the Apostles' Creed.
- discover that Christians believe in Jesus Christ.
- explore why belief in Jesus Christ matters in our lives.

Theme

Christians believe in Jesus.

Bible verse

"She will give birth to a son, and you will call him Jesus, because he will save his people from their sins."

(Matthew 1:21)

Focus for the Teacher

In this second lesson taking a look at what Christians believe, we will be focusing on Jesus. It seems rather obvious to say that Christians believe in Jesus Christ. After all, Christians are followers of Jesus. But there is more to it than simply saying we believe Jesus lived. After all, there is historical evidence for the existence of Jesus. What sets Christianity apart from many other world religions is how we view Jesus. By many other religions, Jesus is considered a prophet and an important teacher. Christians agree that Jesus was a prophet and a teacher. We believe Jesus is also the Son of God.

During Jesus' time on earth, Jesus did things ordinary people could not do. The Gospels tell of the miracles Jesus performed and the people Jesus healed. Additionally, people felt called to follow Jesus. When Jesus asked his original disciples to come and follow him, they did. These fishermen and tax collectors left behind the lives they had known and followed Jesus. They experienced something when they encountered Jesus that made them want to know more. They believed that Jesus was the Christ, God's only Son.

> We believe Jesus is the Son of God.

"God so loved the world...." These familiar words that begin John 3:16 tell us why Jesus, God's Son, spent time on earth. When God wanted to tell us how much we were loved, God sent Jesus. Jesus was sent by God to show us how to live. Jesus showed us a better way—God's way. Jesus taught us about loving each other, caring for the sick and the poor, and working for peace. The name *Jesus* means "Savior." Jesus came to save us by showing us a better way to live and inspiring us to change.

Why does it matter that we believe Jesus is God's Son? Jesus' story is the defining story of the Christian faith. Following Jesus is our purpose in life. We were born to follow in Jesus' footsteps and show God's love to the world. And because of Jesus' resurrection, we know that when our life on earth is over, it is not the end.

Explore Interest Groups

Be sure adult leaders are waiting when the first child arrives. Greet and welcome the children. Get the children involved in an activity that interests them and introduces the theme for the day's activities.

What Is Your Name?

- **Say:** In biblical times, people had only one name. Middle and last names were not used, but instead first names were often followed by identifying information. The information used to identify people might be their relationship to someone else, their job, or where they were from. For example, some people knew Jesus as Jesus son of Joseph. He was also known as Jesus the Carpenter, Jesus of Nazareth, and Jesus the Christ.

- **Ask:** If you were known by your first name and some identifying information, what might your name be?

- Allow children to share their ideas. Remind them that there are multiple possibilities for each person's name.

- Give each child a piece of paper. Invite each child to choose one possible identifying name for himself or herself and use a crayon or marker to write the name in bubble letters or block letters on the paper.

- Encourage each child to decorate his or her name.

Prepare

✓ Provide paper, crayons, and markers.

✓ *Option:* Take a picture of each child holding his or her completed name art. Use the pictures to create a photo gallery of the children in your class.

Names for Jesus

- Give each child a copy of **Reproducible 2a: Names for Jesus** and a pencil.

- **Say:** Jesus was known by many different names. Each of Jesus' names tells something about him.

- Encourage each child to complete the puzzle.

- **Ask:** What is your favorite name for Jesus?

- Allow children an opportunity to respond.

Prepare

✓ Provide copies of **Reproducible 2a: Names for Jesus**.

✓ Supply pencils.

✓ *Answers:* Emmanuel, Son of God, Prince of Peace, Messiah, Savior, Christ, Lord, Counselor, Good Shepherd, Light of the World

Prepare

✓ Identify a large, open area free of obstacles to play the game.

Good News Tag

- **Say:** God sent Jesus to the world to tell people about God's love. We are going to play a game of tag to remind us of the good news Jesus brought to people. If you are tagged, you must sit down and stay in one spot until someone says, "Good news, (*name*), God loves you!" The person must use your name in order to unfreeze you. As you are playing, remember to look for friends who may need your help to rejoin the game.

- Choose a child to be the first tagger. If you have a large class, choose more than one child to be tagger.

- Encourage children to play the game.

Prepare

✓ Provide paper and pencils.

✓ *Option*: You may choose to let the children work in teams of three to four each. Have teams compare their word lists to see which group came up with the most words.

Make New Words

- Give each child a piece of paper and a pencil.

- Have each child write the words *Jesus Christ Son of God* at the top of the paper.

- Encourage each child to make as many new words as possible using only the letters in the words *Jesus Christ Son of God*.

- Let the children compare their word lists.

Prepare

✓ Write the week's Bible verse on a markerboard or a piece of mural paper and place it where it can easily be seen. ("She will give birth to a son, and you will call him Jesus, because he will save his people from their sins." [Matthew 1:21])

Control the Volume of the Bible Verse

- Show the children the Bible verse.

- Invite the children to read the verse with you.

- **Ask:** Who gave birth to a son named Jesus? (Mary)

- **Say:** God told Mary and Joseph to name the baby Jesus. The name *Jesus* means "Savior." God sent Jesus to save people by showing them a better way to live.

- **Say:** Now let's pretend that I am a volume control slider. We will say the verse together three more times. When I am standing over here (move all the way to your right side), the volume needs to be very soft. As I walk across the room, the volume increases and when I am standing over here (move all the way to your left side), the volume is very loud.

- Encourage the children to say the verse with you three more times as you control the volume with your position.

Large Group

Bring all the children together to experience the Bible story. Use a bell to alert the children to the large-group time.

We Believe Rhythm

- **Say:** Today we are talking about our belief in Jesus. Right now we're going to put that belief to a rhythm.
- Have the children stand up.
- **Say:** The rhythm we will be using is one clap, two stomps, one clap, two stomps.
- Encourage the children to practice the rhythm.
- **Say:** Now let's put words to our rhythm. The words are *We believe in Jesus*. We will put one syllable to each clap or stomp.
- Demonstrate the words and rhythm for the children.
- Invite the children to join you in saying the words with the rhythm several times.

Christians Believe in Jesus Christ

- **Say:** We are continuing to talk about what Christians believe. Last week we talked about believing in God. Today we are talking about Jesus.
- Recruit six volunteers to read today's story.
- Give each volunteer a copy of **Reproducible 2b: Christians Believe in Jesus Christ** and assign each reader a part.
- Have the readers stand in front of the class to read the story. Encourage children to speak loudly.
- Thank your volunteers for sharing today's story.
- **Say:** We believe that Jesus lived, but that's not all we believe about Jesus. Some people who are not Christians believe Jesus lived and was a teacher. What's different about Christians is that we believe Jesus is God's Son.

Prepare

✓ Provide copies of **Reproducible 2b: Christians Believe in Jesus Christ**.

Prepare

✓ Write the second part of the Apostles' Creed on a piece of posterboard. You can find the wording at the bottom of this page.

✓ Display the posterboard next to the poster you made last week, where the children will be able to read both of them. Leave the posters up for the duration of the study.

✓ *Note*: Some versions of the creed include the line, "He descended to the dead," or "He descended into hell." This line has been omitted here.

I Believe in Jesus Christ

- **Say:** Last week we began learning about the Apostles' Creed. The Apostles' Creed is one way Christians talk about what we believe.

- **Ask:** What does the first part of the Apostles' Creed say we believe? (We believe in God.)

- **Say:** Today we have been talking about Jesus. Christians are followers of Jesus, so it makes sense that we believe in Jesus. The section of the Apostles' Creed talking about Jesus is the longest section of the creed. This section gives a little summary of Jesus' life and death.

- Show the children the poster you have made for today. Read the words on the poster to the children.

- **Say:** As I did last week, I am going to ask you, "What do you believe?" This week you will respond with the first and second sections of the Apostles' Creed.

- **Ask:** What do you believe?

- Encourage children to respond by reading the first and second parts of the Apostles' Creed.

- Dismiss children to their small groups.

This week's section of the Apostles' Creed:

I believe in Jesus Christ, his only Son, our Lord,
    who was conceived by the Holy Spirit,
    born of the Virgin Mary,
    suffered under Pontius Pilate,
    was crucified, died, and was buried.
    On the third day he rose again;
    he ascended into heaven,
    is seated at the right hand of the Father,
    and will come again to judge the living and the dead.

Small Groups

Divide the children into small groups. You may organize the groups around age levels or around readers and nonreaders. Keep the groups small, with a maximum of ten children in each group. You may need to have more than one group of each age level.

Young Children

- Have the children sit down.
- **Say:** Today we have been talking about Jesus, God's Son. God sent Jesus to teach people how God wants us to live. I am going to read you a list of actions. If the action is something Jesus teaches us to do, jump up and say, "Ding, ding, ding!" If the action is not something Jesus teaches us to do, stay seated and say, "Buzz!"
- Read the following statements to the children, encouraging them to respond appropriately:
  o Pray. (Ding, ding, ding!)
  o Say hurtful words to someone. (Buzz!)
  o Volunteer to help feed people who are hungry. (Ding, ding, ding!)
  o Say mean things about someone when that person isn't around. (Buzz!)
  o Insult your brother or sister. (Buzz!)
  o Help someone who is hurt. (Ding, ding, ding!)
  o Tell someone that you love him. (Ding, ding, ding!)
  o Smile at someone. (Ding, ding, ding!)
  o Ignore someone who is crying. (Buzz!)
  o Praise God. (Ding, ding, ding!)
  o Tell someone God loves her. (Ding, ding, ding!)
- **Say:** I can tell that you know about the things Jesus taught.
- **Ask:** What else did Jesus teach us about how God wants us to live?
- Allow children an opportunity to share their ideas.
- **Say:** As Christians, we say we believe in Jesus, but saying the words is not enough. We also follow Jesus' teachings. Our job as Christians is to follow Jesus' teachings and example. When we do that, we are living as God wants us to live. Jesus also taught that we are to tell other people about God and Jesus.
- **Ask:** What are some ways you can tell other people about God and Jesus?
- Allow children an opportunity to share their ideas.
- **Pray:** God, thank you for loving us so much that you sent Jesus to teach us more about you. Help us to follow Jesus' example to live as you want us to. We believe in you and we believe that Jesus is your Son. Amen.

Prepare

✓ Provide paper and colored pencils.

Older Children

- **Say:** Today we have been talking about believing in Jesus. Right now you are going to make a mind map. A mind map is a fun way to look at thoughts and ideas that go together.

- Give each child a piece of paper. Have each child use a colored pencil to draw a circle in the middle of the paper and write the words *I believe in Jesus* inside the circle.

- **Say:** Think about the words *I believe in Jesus*. Notice what other words or thoughts come into your mind. Draw a line out from the center circle and write the new word or thought. Draw as many lines out from the circle as you wish. You might want to use a different color for each word or thought. Then look at the new words you have written and go through the same steps, using lines to connect related ideas and thoughts. There are no right or wrong answers. This is your mind map.

- Encourage each child to create a mind map.

- Invite the children to share their mind maps with each other.

- **Say:** The story of Jesus is our story as Christians. We remember and celebrate Jesus' life and ministry throughout the year.

- **Ask:** What part of Jesus' life do we remember at Christmas? (Jesus' birth) On Palm Sunday? (Jesus' triumphant ride into Jerusalem) At Easter? (Jesus' resurrection)

- **Say:** We also remember Jesus' life when we are baptized. Jesus was baptized. When we celebrate Communion we remember Jesus sharing the bread and cup with his disciples. Belief in Jesus is an important part of who we are as Christians. But Christians are not simply Jesus believers; we are followers of Jesus.

- **Ask:** What does it mean to follow Jesus? (to follow Jesus' example and teachings) What are the teachings of Jesus that we follow? How is your life different as a follower of Jesus than it would be if you ignored Jesus' teachings?

- Allow children an opportunity to share their thoughts.

- **Say:** The purpose of our life as Christians is to follow in Jesus' footsteps and in doing so to make the world a better place.

- **Pray:** God, thank you for the example of your Son, Jesus. Help us to follow Jesus' example, that we might share your love with everyone we meet. We believe in you and in your son, Jesus. Amen.

Names for Jesus

Decode the following words to discover some names for Jesus.
Hint: A=Z, B=Y, C=X, and so on.

VNNZMFVO

_____

HLM LU TLW

_____

KIRMXV LU KVZXV

_____

NVHHRZS

_____

HZERLI

_____

XSIRHG

_____

OLIW

_____

XLFMHVOLI

_____

TLLW HSVKSVIW

_____

ORTSG LU GSV DLIOW

_____

Christians Believe in Jesus Christ

Friend 1: Well, here we are at church again.

Friend 2: Talking about church stuff.

Friend 3: Last week we talked about the Apostles' Creed.

Friend 4: And what Christians believe.

Friend 5: We believe in God.

Friend 6: What else do Christians believe?

Friend 2: Well, Christians are followers of Jesus, who is God's Son.

Friend 3: While Jesus was on earth, he performed miracles.

Friend 5: Miracles are something only God can do.

Friend 1: Jesus could do miracles because he is God's Son.

Friend 2: Jesus also healed people.

Friend 6: And Jesus taught people about God.

Friend 4: Jesus showed people how God wants us to live.

Friend 6: Why was God's Son sent to earth?

Friend 1: God sent Jesus to show us how much we are loved.

Friend 4: And God wanted us to know there is a better way to live.

Friend 5: Jesus showed us that better way.

Friend 2: He reminded people to care for one another.

Friend 3: And he taught people that we are to love one another.

Friend 2: Because we believe in Jesus, we follow in Jesus' footsteps.

Friend 5: We follow Jesus' teachings.

Friend 3: We share God's love with everyone we can.

Friend 4: We show God's love by our actions.

Friend 1: Christians believe in God and in Jesus.

Friend 6: What else do Christians believe?

Friend 2: Come back next week to find out!

3. The Holy Spirit

Objectives

The children will:
- learn about the Apostles' Creed.
- discover that Christians believe in the Holy Spirit.
- explore why belief in the Holy Spirit matters in their lives.

Theme

Christians believe in the Holy Spirit.

Bible Verse

"You will receive power when the Holy Spirit has come upon you, and you will be my witnesses in Jerusalem, in all Judea and Samaria, and to the end of the earth."

(Acts 1:8)

Focus for the Teacher

So far in our look at what Christians believe, we have discussed God and Jesus. This week we explore the Holy Spirit. Together, God, Jesus, and the Holy Spirit are referred to as the Trinity. The Trinity is the idea that God is "three in one"—Father, Son, and Spirit, or God the Creator, Jesus Christ, and the Holy Spirit. Christians believe in one God. We also believe that God the Father is God, Jesus is God, and the Holy Spirit is God. Don't worry if you don't completely understand the idea of the Trinity. Theologians and scholars have been wrestling with the idea for hundreds of years. The idea of the Trinity will be mentioned in this lesson, but it's OK if children don't fully understand the concept. Part of faith is embracing the mystery of God. God is greater and more complex than human beings can imagine and understand.

> The Holy Spirit is God working within us.

What do we mean when we talk about the Holy Spirit? Throughout the Bible, the Spirit is often referred to as the breath of God. Jesus calls the Spirit the paraclete. The Greek word *paraclete* can be translated as advocate, comforter, or helper. After Jesus' resurrection and before he ascended to heaven, Jesus promised his followers they would receive the Holy Spirit to help them continue Jesus' ministry. It was on the Day of Pentecost that the disciples received the Spirit. On this occasion the Spirit arrived with the rush of wind and the appearance of flames.

The Holy Spirit is God working within us. The Spirit is the presence of God that empowers, leads, and guides us as we seek to do God's work in the world. The wonderful thing about the Holy Spirit is that God is not "out there" or "up there," but within us. It is important to note that the Spirit is already present within each one of us. God is already with us. We have a choice. We can resist God's Spirit or we can welcome the Spirit of God at work in our lives.

How do we recognize the Holy Spirit in our lives? We must actively listen. There are many voices in our lives, telling us what to do. We are surrounded by the voices of other people and societal messages suggesting what we should say, how we should act, who we should associate with, and much more. Each of us decides which voices to listen to. The good news is that God's Spirit never gives up on us and will continue speaking to us and urging us to listen.

Explore Interest Groups

Be sure that adult leaders are waiting when the first child arrives. Greet and welcome each child. Get the children involved in activities that interest them and that introduce the theme for the day's activities.

Holy Spirit Relay

- Divide the children into teams of five to ten each. If you have a small class, have all of the children work together.
- Have each team line up in a lane at the opposite end from a basket.
- **Say:** The baskets at the end of your lanes contain Ping-Pong balls with letters written on them. Each team will send one person at a time over to pick up one ball and bring it back. The next person may not start until the previous person has returned. When you have all of your letters, you will be able to spell the words *Holy Spirit*.
- Ask the children if they understand what they are to do.
- **Say:** There are two more instructions. Once you take the ball out of the basket you must put it on the floor and blow it back to the starting line. The second rule is that you need to collect the letters in the order needed to spell *Holy Spirit*. Think about what letter you need because if you bring back the wrong letter you will need to blow it back to the basket and get the correct letter.
- Encourage the children to play the game.

Prepare

- ✓ Provide Ping-Pong balls and baskets. You will need ten Ping-Pong balls and a basket for each team.
- ✓ Use pool noodles or cardboard boxes as barriers to create lanes. Place tape on the floor to indicate the beginning and ending of each three-to-five-feet wide lane. The number of lanes will depend on the size of your class. You will need to create a lane for each team of five to ten children.
- ✓ Use a permanent marker to make a set of ten balls for each team by writing one letter on each ball to spell "Holy Spirit."
- ✓ Place each set of balls in a basket. Set a basket at the end of each lane.

Breath Painting

- Have the children wear art smocks to protect their clothing.
- Give each child a piece of paper and a straw.
- **Say:** Today you are going to use your breath to paint a picture. I will put paint on your paper. Blow through the straw I have given you to blow the paint around on the paper.
- Let each child choose a color of paint and put some paint on the child's paper.
- Encourage the children to use the straws to gently blow the paint around on the paper.
- Add other colors of paint to the children's papers as they are ready for them.
- Set the paintings aside to dry.
- **Say:** You used your breath to create a painting. Today we are talking about the Holy Spirit. The Spirit is sometimes described as the Breath of God.

Prepare

- ✓ Protect the work surface with paper or plastic table coverings.
- ✓ Provide paper, paint, art smocks, and straws.
- ✓ *Tip*: If your paint is thick, use water to thin it so it will be easier to blow across the paper.

The Spirit Says

- **Say:** Today we are talking about the Holy Spirit. Right now I am going to give you some directions. Do whatever I say, but only if I begin with "The Spirit says." If you don't hear me begin with "The Spirit says," then don't do whatever I am asking you to do.

- Play the game using the following or other commands:
  - o   The Spirit says stand up.
  - o   The Spirit says touch your toes.
  - o   Jump up and down. (Some children will probably start jumping. Do not eliminate children who make a mistake.)
  - o   The Spirit says turn around.
  - o   The Spirit says jump up and down.
  - o   Pat your head.
  - o   The Spirit says stop jumping.
  - o   The Spirit says pretend to wash your hands.
  - o   Reach for the sky.
  - o   The Spirit says wave at your neighbor.
  - o   Give your neighbor a high five.
  - o   The Spirit says sit down.

- As time permits, let the children take turns being the leader and giving "The Spirit says" commands.

Prepare

✓ Provide copies of **Reproducible 3a: Holy Spirit Word Find**.

✓ Supply pencils.

Holy Spirit Word Find

- **Say:** Today we are talking about the Holy Spirit.
- Give each child a copy of **Reproducible 3a: Holy Spirit Word Find** and a pencil.
- Encourage each child to find the words.

Answer Key:

J	E	S	A	D	V	O	C	A	T	E	R
U	S	I	B	E	L	V	E	I	G	O	E
D	O	G	F	O	H	T	A	E	R	B	T
D	T	E	H	F	O	A	T	H	R	E	R
Y	A	L	I	M	L	Y	C	R	E	R	O
O	T	F	H	E	Y	A	R	C	E	N	F
A	N	I	D	E	S	A	E	R	T	H	M
A	I	T	N	S	P	O	P	N	O	G	O
J	D	A	I	I	T	L	H	E	H	C
O	L	Y	S	P	R	I	E	R	I	T	I
N	G	O	D	W	I	T	H	I	N	U	S
T	H	H	O	L	T	Y	C	A	Y	D	E

Large Group

Bring all the children together to experience the Bible story. Use a bell to alert the children to the large-group time.

Cheer for the Holy Spirit

- Lead the children in the following cheer:

  - o **Leader:** Give me an H!
  - o **Children:** H!
  - o **Leader:** Give me an O!
  - o **Children:** O!
  - o **Leader:** Give me an L!
  - o **Children:** L!
  - o **Leader:** Give me a Y!
  - o **Children:** Y!
  - o **Leader:** What does that spell?
  - o **Children:** Holy!
  - o **Leader:** Give me an S!
  - o **Children:** S!
  - o **Leader:** Give me a P!
  - o **Children:** P!

  - o **Leader:** Give me an I!
  - o **Children:** I!
  - o **Leader:** Give me an R!
  - o **Children:** R!
  - o **Leader:** Give me another I!
  - o **Children:** I!
  - o **Leader:** Give me a T!
  - o **Children:** T!
  - o **Leader:** What does that spell?
  - o **Children:** Spirit!
  - o **Leader:** Now put them together!
  - o **Children:** Holy Spirit!
  - o **Leader:** One more time!
  - o **Children:** Holy Spirit!

Christians Believe in the Holy Spirit

- **Say:** We are continuing to talk about what Christians believe. So far we have talked about our belief in God and Jesus. Today we are talking about the Holy Spirit.

- Recruit six volunteers to read today's story.

- Give each volunteer a copy of **Reproducible 3b: Christians Believe in the Holy Spirit** and assign each reader a part.

- Have the readers stand in front of the class to read the story. Encourage children to speak loudly.

- Thank your volunteers for sharing today's story.

- **Say:** Before Jesus left his disciples, he promised to send the Spirit to help them continue to do his ministry. The Holy Spirit is God's presence with us that helps us to do God's work.

Prepare

✓ Provide copies of **Reproducible 3b: Christians Believe in the Holy Spirit.**

Prepare

✓ Write the week's Bible verse on a markerboard or a piece of mural paper and place it where it can easily be seen. ("You will receive power when the Holy Spirit has come upon you, and you will be my witnesses in Jerusalem, in all Judea and Samaria, and to the end of the earth." [Acts 1:8])

Prepare

✓ Write the third part of the Apostles' Creed on a piece of posterboard:

I believe in the Holy Spirit.

✓ Display the posterboard next to the previous two posters where the children will be able to read them. Leave the posters up for the duration of the study.

Emphasizing the Bible Verse

- **Say:** Today's Bible verse is from the Book of Acts.

- Show the children the Bible verse. Invite the children to read the verse with you.

- **Say:** These are Jesus' words to his disciples as he promised the Holy Spirit would help them continue his ministry. We are going to say the Bible verse again. This time, each time we say the word *you*, we will emphasize it. Say the word *you* a little louder than the other words, and say it like you mean it.

- Encourage the children to read the verse and emphasize the word *you*.

- **Say:** We are going to say the verse one more time, again emphasizing the word *you*. This time as we say the verse, imagine Jesus is saying these words to you, personally, and promising you the power of the Spirit.

- Have the children say the verse again as directed.

- **Say:** The Holy Spirit is within each of us.

I Believe in the Holy Spirit

- **Say:** We have been learning about the Apostles' Creed as a way of discussing what Christians believe.

- Show the children the poster you have made for today.

- **Say:** Unlike the section in the creed about Jesus, the section on the Holy Spirit is short. Today when I ask you, "What do you believe?" you will read all three sections of the Apostles' Creed that we have discussed so far.

- **Ask:** What do you believe?

- Encourage children to respond by reading the first three parts of the Apostles' Creed.

- Dismiss children to their small groups.

Small Groups

Divide the children into small groups. You may organize the groups around age levels or around readers and nonreaders. Keep the groups small, with a maximum of ten children in each group. You may need to have more than one group of each age level.

Young Children

- Have the children sit in a circle. Show them the uninflated balloon.

- **Say:** I am going to toss this balloon in the air and I want you to keep it up in the air as long as you can without moving from where you are sitting.

- Toss the balloon up in the air and encourage the children to try and keep it in the air. Try this a couple of times.

- **Ask:** What would make this task easier? (Blowing up the balloon.)

- Blow up the balloon and tie it closed.

- Toss the inflated balloon in the air and encourage the children to keep it in the air.

- **Ask:** Why is it easier to keep the balloon up now? (It has air inside of it.) Can you see the air inside of the balloon? (No.) How do you know the air is there? (We can see that the balloon has expanded.)

- **Say:** We can't see air, but we can see the effect of air on the balloon. I can't see the Holy Spirit either, but I can see the effect of the Holy Spirit. The Holy Spirit is God's presence within us that helps us do God's work. Every time I see one of you doing God's work, I see the effect of the Holy Spirit.

- Give examples of times you have seen the children doing God's work or showing God's love.

- **Ask:** What other ways can you do God's work?

- Allow children an opportunity to share their ideas.

- **Ask:** How do you know what God wants you to do?

- Let children share their ideas.

- **Say:** If we pay attention, the Holy Spirit will help us figure out what God wants us to do. Sometimes the Spirit speaks through other people in our lives. Other times the Spirit speaks inside of us as more of a feeling or nudge. The Spirit can also speak to us through the words of the Bible or when we are praying.

- **Pray:** God, thank you for your Spirit within us, helping us and guiding us. Help us to listen for your Spirit speaking to us and letting us know what you want us to do. Amen.

Prepare
✓ Supply an uninflated balloon.

Prepare

✓ Provide mural paper and markers.

✓ Cut a large piece of mural paper.

Older Children

- Have the children sit in a circle. Place the mural paper in the center of the circle.

- **Say:** There are many voices in our lives trying to tell us what to do. Some of those voices are our parents. Other voices are our friends. Then there are the messages that we get from watching TV or movies or reading. Some voices come from inside of us—things we want to do. Some of the messages we recognize as obviously good ideas, such as, "Do your homework." Other messages we know are not good ideas, such as, "Steal that pack of gum when no one is looking."

- **Ask:** What are some things you are encouraged to do by the different voices in your life? What messages do you get from the voices about what to do?

- Invite children to use markers to write down the messages they receive—things they think of or are encouraged to do—on the mural paper. Encourage children to work together and brainstorm as they write.

- **Say:** That's a lot of messages! Let's take a look at these messages and decide which ones represent things that God would want us to do.

- **Ask:** How do we decide whether God wants us to do something? (Is it something Jesus would do? Is it something the Bible teaches us about? Does it go with the teaching of Jesus even if he didn't speak about it specifically?)

- As a group, look at each message on the paper and decide whether the message is consistent with doing God's work.

- Have the children circle the messages that represent things God would want us to do, and cross out the messages that are not consistent with living as God wants us to live.

- *Note*: Depending on the message, the answer may not be clear-cut. Sometimes a message that is consistent with God's will for one person is not for someone else. Let the children know that the Spirit has different messages for each of us.

- **Say:** The messages that are consistent with the way God wants us to live are the Spirit's voice. The Spirit is the presence of God within us, helping us do God's work.

- **Ask:** What message do you think the Spirit has for you right now about ways you can do God's work?

- Invite children to share, reminding them that sharing is optional.

- **Pray:** God, thank you for the gift of your Spirit that helps us do your work. Help us to pay attention and be aware of the messages your Spirit has for us. Amen.

Creed: Children's Leader Guide

Holy Spirit Word Find

These words are used to talk about the Holy Spirit. Search for the words in the puzzle. They may be forward, backward, up, down, or diagonal.

Advocate	Helper
Breath of God	Holy Spirit
Comforter	Trinity
God Within Us	

```
J  E  S  A  D  V  O  C  A  T  E  R
U  S  I  B  E  L  V  E  I  G  O  E
D  O  G  F  O  H  T  A  E  R  B  T
D  T  E  H  F  O  A  T  H  R  E  R
Y  A  L  I  M  L  Y  C  R  E  R  O
O  T  F  H  E  Y  A  R  C  E  N  F
A  N  I  D  E  S  A  E  R  T  H  M
A  I  T  N  S  P  O  P  N  O  G  O
J  D  A  I  I  I  T  L  H  E  H  C
O  L  Y  S  P  R  I  E  R  I  T  I
N  G  O  D  W  I  T  H  I  N  U  S
T  H  H  O  L  T  Y  C  A  Y  D  E
```

Christians Believe in the Holy Spirit

Friend 1: Here we are again!

Friend 2: At church, talking about church stuff.

Friend 3: This is the third week we've been talking about the Apostles' Creed.

Friend 4: And what Christians believe.

Friend 5: We believe in God and in Jesus.

Friend 6: What else do Christians believe?

Friend 2: Christians also believe in the Holy Spirit.

Friend 6: What's the Holy Spirit?

Friend 4: The Spirit is the presence of God inside of us.

Friend 6: If the Holy Spirit is God inside of us, isn't that just God?

Friend 4: Kind of. The Holy Spirit is part of the Trinity.

Friend 3: Trinity means three, right?

Friend 5: Right. The Trinity is God, Jesus, and Holy Spirit.

Friend 1: So, God the Father, God the Son—that's Jesus—and God the Spirit.

Friend 3: I thought there was only one God.

Friend 2: You're right. But that one God is made up of three parts.

Friend 6: I think that's a little confusing.

Friend 1: Yes, it can be confusing. Just accept that God is a mystery!

Friend 6: So the Holy Spirit…how does it help me do God's work?

Friend 3: The Spirit is that gentle nudge that encourages us to do the right thing.

Friend 5: When we have the courage to do God's work, that's the Spirit at work.

Friend 4: Christians believe in God. Christians believe in Jesus.

Friend 2: And Christians believe in the Holy Spirit.

Friend 6: What else do Christians believe?

Friend 5: Come back next week to find out!

4. The Church and the Communion of Saints

Objectives	Theme
The children will: • learn about the Apostles' Creed. • discover that Christians believe in the church and the communion of saints. • explore why belief in the church matters in their lives.	Christians practice their beliefs in community. **Bible verse** Jesus said to them again, "Peace be with you. As the Father sent me, so I am sending you." (John 20:21)

Focus for the Teacher

The first three lessons in this study of what Christians believe have looked at the Trinity—God, Jesus, and the Holy Spirit. This week we explore our belief in "the holy catholic church" and "the communion of saints." Before we explore this belief, a few words about the words themselves. The word *holy* means belonging to God. The word *catholic*, as used here with a lowercase *c*, is an adjective meaning "universal." It does not refer to the Roman Catholic Church, at least not exclusively. When we confess our belief in the "holy catholic church," we are saying we believe in God's universal church—God's people working together throughout the world.

The word *saint* as used in the phrase "the communion of saints" does not refer only to those canonized by the church such as St. Peter and St. Francis. Rather it refers to all Christians. A saint is one who is set apart for God. All followers of Christ are called to be saints, or at least to work toward being saints.

What does it mean to say we believe in the church? When the Apostle Peter wrote to encourage early Christians who were suffering because of their belief in Christ, he said, "Once you weren't a people, but now you are God's people" (1 Peter 2:10). The church is God's people. The church is a family of people working together to figure out how to follow Jesus and do God's work in the world.

When Jesus was on the earth, he didn't attempt his ministry alone. He called people to follow and to help him. And then he sent his followers into the world to continue his ministry, not individually but together. Christianity is a group activity. The Apostle Paul described the church as the body of Christ, all parts working together. We can do more of God's work when we work together. Every part of the body of Christ is important. The church needs you, and you need the church.

> The church is God's people.

Creed: Children's Leader Guide

Explore Interest Groups

Be sure that adult leaders are waiting when the first child arrives. Greet and welcome each child. Get the children involved in activities that interest them and that introduce the theme for the day's activities.

Water Glass Instrument

- Give each child a glass.

- Pour some water into each child's glass, pouring different amounts into each glass.

- Give each child a metal spoon. Show the children how to gently tap the metal spoon on the side of the glass to produce a sound.

- **Ask:** Does each glass make the same sound? Why do you think the glasses produce different sounds?

- Challenge the children to put the glasses in order from highest sound to lowest sound.

- Encourage the children to experiment and see if they can work together to play a scale or a familiar tune.

- Encourage the children to experiment with playing "chords" by having two or more children tap their glasses at the same time.

- **Ask:** Could any of you play a tune with only your glass? (Maybe, but it would have only one note!)

- **Say:** When we put all the glasses together we can make more complex and interesting music. The church is like this too. One person can do God's work. But when we work together we can do more of God's work, in ways we couldn't do if working alone.

Prepare

✓ Provide drinking glasses (not plastic), pitchers for water, and metal spoons. You will need a glass and a spoon for each child.

✓ Fill the pitchers half-full with water.

✓ *Note*: If you have a large class, divide children into groups of six to eight each for this activity.

Church Language

- **Say:** You may have noticed that in the church we sometimes use fancy language that you wouldn't use every day. In some cases, the church has been using these phrases for hundreds of years. At times it can be challenging to understand what is being said.

- Give each child a copy of **Reproducible 4a: Discover the Phrase**.

- Encourage each child to solve the puzzle.

- **Ask:** Have you ever heard the phrase "communion of saints"?

- **Say:** When we talk about the communion of saints, we are referring to all Christians, past and present, even those who haven't been born yet. If you hear a word or phrase at church that you don't understand, ask someone what it means. That person may not know either, but then you can find out together.

Prepare

✓ Provide copies of **Reproducible 4a: Discover the Phrase**.

✓ Supply pencils.

✓ *Answer*: Communion of saints

Prepare

✓ Supply paper sacks and a variety of potential building materials such as paper, straws, tape, string, paper clips, craft sticks, aluminum foil, cardboard, and plastic lids.

✓ Prepare paper sacks that contain a variety of potential building materials, making sure each sack contains the same supplies. You will need a sack for each group of four to six children.

Prepare

✓ Supply mural paper and markers.

✓ Cut a large piece of mural paper. At the top of the paper, write "Our Church Helps People."

✓ Spend some time thinking about your church's ministries so you can help the children as they are making this list.

Build a Church

• Divide the class into groups of four to six children each.

• Give each group of children a paper sack.

• **Say:** As a group, I would like you to use the items in the sack I have given you to build a church.

• Encourage the children to work together and build their churches.

• After a set amount of time, have the children admire all the churches.

• **Say:** You have all done a great job of using the supplies you had to build a church. As wonderful as your churches are, they are all missing one very important thing.

• **Ask:** Can you think of something your churches are missing that is important in order for a church to do God's work? (people)

• **Say:** When we say the word *church*, we often think of a church building. While our buildings help us do ministry, they are not as important as the people of a church. A church needs people to be able to do God's work.

Our Church Helps People

• **Ask:** What is a church?

• Allow children to share their ideas about what church is.

• **Say:** A church is a group of people who are Christians together. The people of a church do many things together, including learning, worshiping, and helping people. Right now let's make a list of all the things we can think of that our church does to help people. This can include ways the church helps our members, such as providing a place to worship and learn together, and ways that members of our church help people outside our church.

• Invite the children to think of as many ministries of the church as they can.

• Write the children's ideas on the mural paper.

• **Say:** Wow! Our church does a lot of ministry and helps a lot of people. No one person could do all these things by himself or herself. It's a good thing we have one another and can work together to do God's work.

• Save the list of ministries to be used during small-group time with the older children.

Large Group

Bring all the children together to experience the Bible story. Use a bell to alert the children to the large-group time.

"We Are the Church"

- Teach the children the words to the chorus of the song "We Are the Church."
- **Say**: Now we are going to add some actions to go along with the words. Each time we sing the word "church," tent your hands over your head as if forming a roof.
- Encourage the children to practice the action for the word *church*.
- **Say**: When you sing the word "I" point to yourself. When you sing the word "you" point to someone else. When you sing the word "we" point back and forth between yourself and other people. As we sing the line, "All who follow Jesus, all around the world!" we will walk in place.
- Invite the children to sing the chorus while doing the actions.
- Teach the children the first verse of the song "We Are the Church."
- **Say**: During the verse, we will continue to tent our hands over our heads each time we sing the word "church." We will also add actions to the following words.
- Teach the children actions to accompany the following words:
  - o building ((Pretend to hammer one fist on top of the other)
  - o steeple ((Tent your hands over your head as if forming a steep roof)
  - o resting place ((Lay your head on your hands as if sleeping)
  - o people (Point to yourself and others)
- Invite the children to sing the chorus, the first verse, and then the chorus again while doing the actions.

Prepare

✓ Review the song "We Are the Church" and the actions described below, so you can teach them to the children.If you are not familiar with the tune, it can be found online.

✓ If you are not familiar with the tune, it can be found online.

Prepare

✓ Provide copies of **Reproducible 4b: Christians Believe in the Church and the Communion of Saints**.

Christians Believe in the Church and the Communion of Saints

- **Say:** We are continuing to talk about what Christians believe. We've talked about our belief in God, Jesus, and the Holy Spirit. Today we are talking about the church.

- Recruit six volunteers to read today's story.

- Give each volunteer a copy of **Reproducible 4b: Christians Believe in the Church and the Communion of Saints** and assign each reader a part.

- Have the readers stand in front of the class to read the story. Encourage children to speak loudly.

- Thank your volunteers for sharing today's story.

- **Say:** There is a phrase the church uses to talk about all Christians—past Christians, current Christians, and Christians who haven't been born yet. Some of you solved a puzzle earlier to discover this phrase.

- **Ask:** What is the phrase sometimes used to talk about all Christians? (communion of saints)

- **Say:** When we use the phrase "communion of saints," we are talking about all Christians. It's another way to say we are all working together to do God's work. We are continuing the work done by Christians who lived before us, and know God's work will be continued by future Christians.

Prepare

✓ Write the week's Bible verse on a markerboard or a piece of mural paper and place it where it can easily be seen. (Jesus said to them again, "Peace be with you. As the Father sent me, so I am sending you." [John 20:21])

Discuss the Bible Verse

- **Say:** Today's Bible verse is from the Gospel of John.

- Show the children the Bible verse.

- Invite the children to read the verse with you.

- **Ask:** Who do you think Jesus was speaking these words to? (his disciples)

- **Say:** Jesus spoke these words to his disciples when he appeared to them after he had been raised from the dead.

- **Ask:** What do you think Jesus was sending the disciples to do? (to continue his ministry, to tell people about God, to do God's work)

- **Say:** Jesus sent his disciples to continue to do the work he had started. They were to tell people about God and teach them how God wanted them to live. They were also to help people like Jesus did.

- **Ask:** Who continues this work today? (We do.)

- **Say:** When we are following Jesus and doing God's work, we are continuing the ministry of Jesus and his disciples.

- Invite the children to read the verse with you again.

I Believe in the Church and the Communion of Saints

- **Say:** The Apostles' Creed helps Christians remember and talk about the things we believe. Today we are adding to the creed the words "the holy catholic church, the communion of saints." The word *catholic* as used here doesn't mean the Roman Catholic Church. When written with a lowercase *c* like it is here, it is a word that means "universal" or "everywhere." The "holy catholic church" means God's people all around the world working together. We've already discussed that the "communion of saints" means all Christians. Today when I ask you, "What do you believe?" you will respond by reading all four posters.

- **Ask:** What do you believe?

- Encourage children to respond by reading the first four parts of the Apostles' Creed.

- Dismiss children to their small groups.

Prepare

✓ Write the following words on a piece of posterboard:

> the holy catholic church, the communion of saints,

✓ Display the posterboard next to the previous Apostles' Creed posters, where the children will be able to read them. Leave the posters up for the duration of the study.

Small Groups

Divide the children into small groups. You may organize the groups around age levels or around readers and nonreaders. Keep the groups small, with a maximum of ten children in each group. You may need to have more than one group of each age level.

Prepare

✓ Cut a large piece of mural paper.

✓ Supply markers.

Young Children

- Have the children sit in a circle. Place the mural paper in the center.
- **Say:** As followers of Jesus, we continue what Jesus started.
- **Ask:** What are some ways we continue what Jesus started?
- Allow children an opportunity to share their ideas.
- **Say:** Jesus told people God loves them. We do, too, as we continue Jesus' work. We tell people and sbow people that God loves them.
- Write the word *you* in the center of the mural paper.
- **Ask:** How many people do you think you could tell God loves them?
- Allow children an opportunity to respond.
- **Say:** Even if you told everybody you know that God loves them, there would be a limit to the number of people you could tell.
- Draw a circle around the word *you*, leaving room for children to write their names inside the circle.
- Invite each child to write his or her name inside the circle.
- **Ask:** What if we all worked together? Would we be able to tell more people about God's love than any one of us alone could?
- **Say:** Together, our group could tell more people about God, but there would still be a limit to how many people we could tell.
- Draw a larger circle around the circle of names. In this circle write the words *our church*.
- **Ask:** What if everyone in our church told people God loves them? How many people would we be able to tell about God's love then?
- Draw a bigger circle around the previous circles. In this circle write the words *churches in our country*.
- **Ask:** What if all Christians in our country told people God loves them? Would we be able to share God's love with more people?
- Draw one last circle around all of the previous circles. In this circle write the words *churches all around the world*.
- **Ask:** What if we include Christians all around the world? How many people could we tell about God's love then?
- **Say:** When we work together as the church, we are able to do so much more than any one of us could do by ourselves.
- **Pray:** God, thank you for loving us. We want to share your love with others. Help us to work together as your church to continue Jesus' ministry and do your work. Amen.

Older Children

- **Say:** Earlier, some of you helped make a list of ministries our church does that help people.

- Invite children to look over the list.

- **Say:** Jesus sent his disciples into the world to continue his ministry. As Jesus' followers, we are also to continue Jesus' ministry.

- **Ask:** Do you think these ministries continue the work Jesus did when he was on earth? Why or why not?

- Allow children an opportunity to share their thoughts.

- **Ask:** Are there any ways our church does Jesus' ministry that you do not see on this list?

- Have children add any additional ministries they can think of.

- **Ask:** Are there any other ways our church could be continuing Jesus' ministry that we aren't doing right now?

- Invite children to add new ministry ideas to the list.

- **Say:** That's a lot of ministry. There is a lot of God's work represented on this sheet of paper.

- **Ask:** Could any single one of you do all of this ministry by yourself? (No.)

- **Say:** God's work gets done when we all work together. Today we are going to decide on a ministry we can do together. It could be something on this list. It could be one of the new ministry ideas we came up with. Or maybe it's something we haven't thought of yet.

- Invite the children to come up with ideas for possible ministries that your group could do together, referring them to the ministry list for ideas.

- Remind the children that all ideas are welcome.

- As a group, discuss the ideas and choose one you would like to pursue.

- **Ask:** What would we need to do to participate in or begin this ministry? What will we need to do first? What will we need to do next?

- Make a plan to implement your group's ministry project.

- **Say:** Working together, we can do God's work. That's what the church does.

Prepare

✓ Use the list of your church's ministries made earlier in the lesson. If you have multiple groups of older children, display the list where all groups can see it.

Discover the Phrase

There is a phrase the church uses to describe all Christians—past, present, and future. This phrase refers to all the Christians who have done God's work since Jesus' time, all Christians alive and doing God's work now, and even those Christians who haven't been born yet.

Solve the puzzle below, writing each letter on the line provided. When you are finished, read down to discover the phrase.

You will find me twice in cocoa, but only once in Christian. _____

I am in octopus and open, but not in purple. _____

You'll find me twice in the middle of commit. _____

I start moor but finish up room. _____

I am in fun and furniture, but not in fine. _____

I am exactly in the middle of crinkle. _____

I'm a vowel, but you won't find me in the word computable. _____

Look for me twice in cuckoo, but only once in clock. _____

You'll find me in banana and nail and land, but not in baby. _____

I am the only vowel in tomorrow. _____

I'm at the end of cuff and the beginning of freeze. _____

I am in the middle and end of geysers. _____

I am a vowel found in beautiful but not in equinoxes. _____

Look for me in fire and ice and wind. _____

I am found in cinnamon but not in calm or ratio. _____

Look for me in apostle and thistle, but not in disciple. _____

You'll find me in the middle of Frisbee. _____

Christians Believe in the Church and the Communion of Saints

Friend 1: Here we are at church again.

Friend 2: Guess what we're talking about today.

Friend 3: The Apostles' Creed? What Christians believe?

Friend 6: Right! Christians believe in God, Jesus, and the Holy Spirit.

Friend 4: Christians also believe in the church.

Friend 3: The church? You mean like the building we're in right now?

Friend 5: Not exactly. The church is more than a building.

Friend 3: That's true! The church is people.

Friend 5: The earliest Christians didn't have a church. They met in homes.

Friend 2: So the church is Christians, working together to do God's work in the world.

Friend 6: So when we say we believe in the church, we're saying we believe in people?

Friend 1: Kind of. We're saying that working together to do God's work is important.

Friend 4: Sort of. We're saying the church is a family of people who care for each other, and that's a good thing.

Friend 3: Does that mean you can't be a Christian by yourself?

Friend 5: You can try, but it's better to be a Christian in a community of people.

Friend 2: People in the church learn together and care for one another.

Friend 5: Together we can do more than any one of us can do alone.

Friend 1: The Apostle Paul described the church as the body of Christ.

Friend 4: Each one of us is an important part of the body of Christ.

Friend 2: The church needs you, and you, and you. And you need the church!

Friend 3: That makes sense.

Friend 6: Working together to do God's work is better than trying to be a Christian alone.

Friend 1: Sounds like you believe in the church!

Friend 6: God, Jesus, the Holy Spirit, and the church—is that all Christians believe?

Friend 2: No, there's more! Come back next week to find out!

5. The Forgiveness of Sins

Objectives

The children will:
- learn about the Apostles' Creed.
- discover that Christians believe in the forgiveness of sins.
- explore why the forgiveness of sins matters.

Theme

Christians believe in forgiveness.

Bible Verse

"Forgive us for the ways we have wronged you, just as we also forgive those who have wronged us."

(Matthew 6:12)

Focus for the Teacher

We affirm our belief in the Trinity—in God who created the world; in Jesus Christ, God's Son; and in the Holy Spirit, God at work within us. We affirm our belief in the church. We remind ourselves that working together is a better way to do God's work than trying to go it alone. Regardless of how often we affirm these things, the fact remains that we all occasionally fall short in our attempts to live as God wants us to live. How reassuring it is to be able to say we believe in the forgiveness of sins.

In Galatians 5:22-23, Paul describes the fruit of the Spirit as "love, joy, peace, patience, kindness, goodness, faithfulness, gentleness, and self-control." These characteristics are evident in those persons who are living Spirit-filled lives.

As followers of Jesus, that should be all of us! But let's be honest. Who among us is loving 100 percent of the time? Who among us is always joyful, every hour of every day? Is there anyone who succeeds in always living in peace with every other person? We could go through Paul's entire list. The truth is that as humans, we make mistakes. We sin.

> The good news is that God forgives!

The good news is that God forgives! No matter how often we fall short of doing God's will, God forgives us. In fact, God has already forgiven us. God's grace is awesome. God loves us, has always loved us, and will never stop loving us. Knowing God's unfailing love for us, we can be assured of God's forgiveness. Does that mean we can do whatever we want, as long as we tell God afterward that we're sorry? Of course not. With the reassurance of God's love and forgiveness comes the responsibility of trying to do better. Because we are forgiven, we try again.

Of course, we are not the only ones God forgives. Everyone else is forgiven too. Jesus taught the disciples to pray, "Forgive us for the ways we have wronged you, just as we also forgive those who have wronged us" (Matthew 6:12). Part of the responsibility of being a forgiven people is forgiving others. We know this isn't always easy. When we feel we have been wronged, we want to stay mad at the one who hurt us. Jesus reminds us to forgive. When we fail at forgiving others, God forgives us, and we try harder.

Explore Interest Groups

Be sure that adult leaders are waiting when the first child arrives. Greet and welcome each child. Get the children involved in activities that interest them and that introduce the theme for the day's activities.

Spell It Out

- Show the children the letters you have written on the piece of paper.
- **Say:** Today I want you to find these letters.
- Encourage the children to look through the magazines and cut out the letters E, F, G, I, O, R, and V. The letters may be any size, color, or style.
- Have children cut out multiple copies of each letter.
- **Say:** We are going to use these letters to spell an important word.
- **Ask:** Can you guess what the word is?
- **Say:** The word we are going to spell uses each of these letters one time. The word is *forgive*.
- **Ask:** What does *forgive* mean? (to let go of angry or hurt feelings when someone has done something wrong)
- Invite children to use the cut-out letters to spell the word *forgive*, gluing the letters in order on the mural paper or posterboard.
- Have children keep working to spell the word *forgive* as many times as they can.

Prepare

✓ Cut a large piece of mural paper or provide a piece of posterboard.

✓ Provide magazines, scissors, and glue sticks.

✓ Write the following letters on a piece of paper: E F G I O R V.

✓ *Note*: Look through the magazines and remove any pages that contain inappropriate pictures or articles.

Let It Go

- Divide the children into groups. The number of groups will depend on the number of backpacks you have.
- Give each group a book-filled backpack.
- Have one child in each group put the backpack on.
- Encourage each child wearing a backpack to do twenty-five jumping jacks while their remaining group members count for them.
- Let each child take a turn doing twenty-five jumping jacks while wearing the backpack.
- **Say:** Now you are all going to do another twenty-five jumping jacks. This time you are going to do the jumping jacks without wearing a backpack.
- Count aloud while the children do twenty-five jumping jacks.
- **Ask:** Was it easier to do the jumping jacks with the backpack on or off? When you were jumping with the backpack on, did you want to stop and take it off?

Prepare

✓ Provide backpacks and heavy books.

✓ Place a few heavy books in each backpack.

✓ *Note*: Be careful not to make the backpacks so heavy that children might hurt their backs.

- **Say:** Today we are talking about forgiveness.
- **Ask:** How do you feel when someone has been unkind to you? Is it easy to forgive that person?
- **Say:** When someone does something wrong that hurts us, we may feel mad or sad. If we hang on to those angry or hurt feelings, it can start to weigh us down, just like the backpacks did. We could start to feel angry all the time. Jesus teaches us that we should forgive those who wrong us. That doesn't mean we won't ever feel angry, sad, or hurt, but we need to try to let those feelings go and forgive.

Prepare

✓ Form a circle of chairs facing inward, using one less chair than the number of children playing the game.

God Forgives

- **Say:** Today we are talking about forgiveness. God loves us, and God forgives us when we make mistakes.
- Choose one child to stand in the center of the circle of chairs. Have the rest of the children sit in the chairs.
- Explain the following rules to the children:
  o The person in the center will say, "God forgives…" and complete the statement by saying something that is true about him or her. For example: "God forgives people wearing red," "God forgives people who have an older brother," or "God forgives people whose favorite food is pizza."
  o Every person in the circle for whom that statement is true must get up and find a new seat at least two chairs away from where they were sitting while the person in the middle tries to get a seat also.
  o The person left standing becomes the next person to deliver a message.
  o If the person in the middle says, "God forgives everyone!" then everyone must move to a new seat.
- Encourage the children to play the game.

Prepare

✓ Provide copies of **Reproducible 5a: Bible Verse Poster**.

✓ Supply crayons and markers.

Bible Verse Poster

- **Say:** Today we are talking about forgiveness.
- Give each child a copy of **Reproducible 5a: Bible Verse Poster**.
- **Say:** Today's Bible verse is an important reminder that we are to forgive others just as God forgives us.
- Invite each child to decorate the Bible verse poster with crayons or markers.
- **Say:** When you take your poster home, hang it where it will remind you about forgiveness.

Large Group

Bring the children together to experience the Bible story. Use a bell to alert the children to the large-group time.

Reassurance and Responsibility

- Show the children the chart you have made.
- **Ask**: What does *reassurance* mean? (to be certain of)
- Under the word *Reassurance* on the mural paper, write "God loves you no matter what!"
- **Say**: Because God loves us, God forgives us when we make mistakes.
- Write the words *God forgives us* in the Reassurance column.
- **Say**: That's reassuring, because we do make mistakes.
- **Ask**: If God loves us no matter what we do, and forgives us, does that mean it's OK to do whatever we want? (No.) Why not? (We thank God for loving us by living as God wants us to live.)
- **Say**: Being a follower of Jesus comes with responsibility.
- **Ask**: What is *responsibility*? (having certain obligations) What responsibilities do you have in your family?
- Let the children respond.
- **Ask**: What responsibilities do we have because we are Christians and are following Jesus?
- Write the children's answers on the mural paper under the word *Responsibility*.

Christians Believe in the Forgiveness of Sins

- **Say**: In our study of what Christians believe, we have talked about believing in God, Jesus, the Holy Spirit, and the church. Today we are talking about forgiveness.
- Recruit six volunteers to read today's story.
- Give each volunteer a copy of **Reproducible 5b: Christians Believe in the Forgiveness of Sins**, and assign each reader a part.
- Have the readers stand in front of the class to read the story. Encourage children to speak loudly.
- Thank your volunteers for sharing today's story.
- **Say**: We believe God forgives our sins. That's reassuring, because we are human and we make mistakes. We also believe that we are to forgive each other. That isn't always easy, but it's important.

Prepare

✓ Cut a large sheet of mural paper and tape it to the wall where the children can easily see it.

✓ Draw a vertical line down the middle of the paper. At the top of the left-hand column write the word *Reassurance*. At the top of the right-hand column write the word *Responsibility*.

Prepare

✓ Provide copies of **Reproducible 5b: Christians Believe in the Forgiveness of Sins**.

Prepare

✓ Write the week's Bible verse on a markerboard or a piece of mural paper and place it where it can easily be seen. ("Forgive us for the ways we have wronged you, just as we also forgive those who have wronged us." [Matthew 6:12])

Prepare

✓ Write the following words on a piece of posterboard:

the forgiveness of sins,

✓ Display the posterboard next to the previous Apostles' Creed posters, where the children will be able to read them. Leave the posters up for the duration of the study.

Back and Forth Bible Verse

- **Say:** Today's Bible verse is part of the Lord's Prayer, the prayer Jesus taught his disciples.

- Show the children the Bible verse.

- Invite the children to read the verse with you.

- Divide the children into three groups.

- **Say:** I will invite one group to start the Bible verse, and you will say the first part of the verse, "Forgive us for the ways we have wronged you." The other two groups will finish the verse by saying, "just as we also forgive those who have wronged us."

- Take turns inviting each group to begin the Bible verse, and encourage the other groups to finish the verse.

I Believe in the Forgiveness of Sins

- **Say:** We have been using the Apostles' Creed to discuss what Christians believe. Today we are adding "the forgiveness of sins." We believe God forgives us when we make mistakes. We also believe God wants us to forgive others when they make mistakes. Today when I ask you "What do you believe?" you will respond by reading from all five posters.

- **Ask:** What do you believe?

- Encourage children to respond by reading the first five parts of the Apostles' Creed.

- Dismiss children to their small groups.

Small Groups

Divide the children into small groups. You may organize the groups around age levels or around readers and nonreaders. Keep the groups small, with a maximum of ten children in each group. You may need to have more than one group of each age level.

Younger and Older Children

- **Say:** Today we have been talking about forgiveness.
- **Ask:** Do you ever need forgiveness? Do you ever make mistakes? Do you ever do something you know God would not want you to do?
- **Say:** We all make mistakes sometimes. We all need to ask for forgiveness. When we make a mistake, it is important to apologize. If our actions have hurt someone, we need to tell that person we're sorry. It's also important to tell God we're sorry, and we can tell God we are going to try to do better.
- **Ask:** Is it easy to apologize?
- **Say:** Sometimes we are the ones who have been wronged and we need to forgive others for hurting us. That's not easy either.
- Give each child a tray of sand.
- **Say:** We are going to spend some time praying for forgiveness. We have all done things we shouldn't have done. As you pray, use your finger to write your "I'm sorry" prayer in the sand. Then wipe the sand clean as a sign of a fresh start. You can write in the sand and wipe it clean as many times as necessary. These prayers are between you and God. God will always forgive you.
- Encourage the children to spend time praying.
- **Say:** Now take some time to pray about forgiving others. If there is someone who has done something wrong to you or whom you are mad at, write his or her name in the sand and then wipe the sand clean as you ask God to help you forgive that person.
- Allow time for the children to pray.
- **Pray:** God, thank you for always loving us, no matter what. It isn't easy to admit, but we make mistakes and don't always live as you want us to. Thank you for forgiving us. Help us to forgive those who have wronged us, just as you have forgiven us. Amen.

Prepare

- ✓ *Note:* Although all children are doing the same activities in their small groups this week, the level of discussion will vary according to the age of children in each group.
- ✓ Supply shallow trays and sand.
- ✓ Pour sand in the bottom of each tray. Make a tray of sand for each child.
- ✓ *Tip:* Have the children sit on a large plastic tablecloth or a large sheet during this activity, to make cleanup of any spilled sand easier.

Bible Verse Poster

"Forgive us for the ways we have wronged you, just as we also forgive those who have wronged us."

(Matthew 6:12)

Christians Believe in the Forgiveness of Sins

Friend 1: Here we are again! Talking about the Apostles' Creed.

Friend 3: And what Christians believe.

Friend 4: We believe in God, the creator of the world.

Friend 5: We believe in Jesus, God's Son.

Friend 6: We believe in the Holy Spirit, God at work within us.

Friend 2: And we believe in the church—Christians working together to do God's work.

Friend 6: What else do Christians believe?

Friend 4: Christians believe in the forgiveness of sins.

Friend 3: Sin. I don't really like to think about sin.

Friend 5: But we all sin. When we don't do what God wants us to do, that's a sin.

Friend 4: Jesus showed us how God wants us to live. We should love each other.

Friend 1: The Apostle Paul said we should show love, joy, peace, patience…

Friend 2: …kindness, goodness, faithfulness, gentleness, and self-control.

Friend 6: I don't always act kindly. And sometimes I lose my temper.

Friend 4: No matter how hard we try, we don't always live like God wants us to.

Friend 3: Well, that's not good, is it?

Friend 5: The good news is that God forgives us. God loves us and will never stop.

Friend 3: So when we make mistakes, God forgives us, right?

Friend 1: Right! But there's more to it than God forgiving us. We need to forgive others.

Friend 5: Wow, that's not always easy.

Friend 4: No, it isn't easy. But it's important.

Friend 2: What happens if we aren't able to forgive someone who has hurt us?

Friend 3: God will forgive us for that too.

Friend 5: And then we try again to forgive.

Friend 6: Is there anything else Christians believe?

Friend 1: Come back next week and find out!

6. The Resurrection of the Body

Objectives

The children will:
- learn about the Apostles' Creed.
- discover that Christians believe in the resurrection of the body.
- explore why belief in the resurrection of the body matters in their lives.

Theme

Christians believe in eternal life.

Bible verse

"Because I live, you will live too."
(John 14:19b)

Focus for the Teacher

This is the final lesson in our study of what Christians believe. We have used the Apostles' Creed to shape our study of Christian beliefs. The Apostles' Creed has been around for hundreds of years. In its present form the Creed has been around since the 400s, but an earlier form of the creed was around in the second or third century. Thus, the Apostles' Creed represents the attempts of early Christians to verbalize important Christian beliefs. When it was first written, the Apostles' Creed was used by persons wishing to be baptized as a way of confessing their Christian faith. The Apostles' Creed has withstood the test of time and is still used today.

In previous lessons we have discussed belief in God, Jesus, the Holy Spirit, the church, and the forgiveness of sins. In today's lesson we will discuss resurrection. When you think about it, this is a relatively short list of things considered as essential beliefs. Certainly Christians have spent much time discussing and deliberating over many beliefs that are not included in the Apostles' Creed. When we

> **Jesus' death was not the final word.**

find ourselves arguing over beliefs, it might be wise to think back on the words given to us by the early Christian church in the form of the Apostles' Creed. Is it necessary for Christians to agree on all our beliefs? Or is it possible to agree on the important beliefs and agree to disagree on other things?

The final section of the Apostles' Creed affirms belief in the resurrection of the body and the life everlasting. Christians know that Jesus was crucified on the cross. However, Jesus' death was not the final word. On Easter morning, the tomb where Jesus' body had been laid was empty. Jesus was raised from the dead and is alive! Jesus appeared to his followers after his resurrection. The New Testament Scriptures contain accounts of people who encountered the risen Christ.

Because of Easter, Christians believe that death does not have the final word. We do not know exactly what life after death looks like. But we believe in Jesus' promise, "Because I live, you will live too" (John 14:19b).

Explore Interest Groups

Be sure that adult leaders are waiting when the first child arrives. Greet and welcome each child. Get the children involved in activities that interest them and that introduce the theme for the day's activities.

Decorate a Cross

- Give each child a piece of paper and have them follow these instructions. You may want to have older children help younger children.
  - o Fold the paper in half, bringing the long sides together.
  - o With the paper still folded, fold over one short edge of the paper, folding over about the top third of the paper and lining up the folded edges.
  - o Leaving the paper folded and with the folded edges to the left and top, use a pencil to draw a line about one inch from the long folded edge of the paper, starting at the bottom and stopping one inch before reaching the top.
  - o Draw another line about one inch from the top folded edge, beginning at the right edge and stopping one inch short of the left edge. The two lines should meet, forming an upside-down "L."
  - o Cut along the pencil line.
  - o Unfold the paper.
- **Ask:** What shape did you cut out of the paper? (a cross)
- **Say:** The cross is a familiar Christian symbol. It reminds us that Jesus died on the cross. The cross is empty because of the Resurrection. The empty cross reminds us that Jesus conquered death and is alive.
- Invite the children to use white crayons to draw designs on their crosses.
- Have each child paint his or her cross, noticing that the crayon resists the paint.
- Allow the crosses to dry.

Prepare
- ✓ Supply paper, scissors, pencils, white crayons, watercolor paints, paintbrushes, and plastic containers for water.
- ✓ Protect the work area with plastic table coverings or newspaper.
- ✓ Fill plastic containers one-third full with water and place them in the center of the table with the watercolor paints.

The Resurrection of the Body

Prepare

✓ Provide copies of **Reproducible 6a: Creed Cards,** copied onto cardstock.

✓ Supply scissors.

Prepare

✓ Supply paper and pencils.

Concentrate on the Creed

- **Say:** Today is our last day talking about the Apostles' Creed and what Christians believe. This game will help you review what we've been talking about.

- Invite each child to find a partner.

- Give each child a copy of **Reproducible 6a: Creed Cards** and a pair of scissors.

- Have the children cut out the cards. Have the pairs of children shuffle their cards together to form a twelve-card deck.

- Explain to the children that they will use the cards to play concentration.

- Have each pair of children lay their cards out facedown between them.

- **Say:** Take turns playing the game. When it is your turn, flip over two cards. If the cards do not match, turn them back over and your turn is over. If you find two cards that match, you get another turn.

- Invite the children to play the game.

Acrostic Poem

- Give each child a piece of paper and a pencil.

- Have each child write the word *Resurrection* vertically down the left side of his or her paper.

- Encourage each child to think of words or phrases about Jesus that begin with the letters in *Resurrection*, and write them next to the appropriate letter.

- Encourage children to share their acrostics with one another.

Large Group

Bring all the children together to experience the Bible story. Use a bell to alert the children to the large-group time.

Cheer for the Good News

- **Say:** Today we are talking about the Resurrection. After Jesus died on the cross, he was raised from the dead. Jesus' resurrection was good news for his followers who thought his death was the end. Let's say a cheer for the good news.

- Lead the children in the following cheer:

    - **Leader:** I say "Good," you say "News." Good!
    - **All:** News!
    - **Leader:** Good!
    - **All:** News!
    - **Leader:** You say "Good," I say "News."
    - **All:** Good!
    - **Leader:** News! Say it again!
    - **All:** Good!
    - **Leader:** News!

Christians Believe in the Resurrection of the Body

- **Say:** This is our final week talking about what Christians believe.

- Recruit six volunteers to read today's story.

- Give each volunteer a copy of **Reproducible 6b: Christians Believe in the Resurrection of the Body** and assign each reader a part.

- Have the readers stand in front of the class to read the story. Encourage children to speak loudly.

- Thank your volunteers for sharing today's story.

- **Say:** We believe in Jesus' resurrection. We also believe in Jesus' promise of eternal life.

Prepare

✓ Provide copies of **Reproducible 6b: Christians Believe in the Resurrection of the Body**.

Prepare

✓ Write the week's Bible verse on a markerboard or a piece of mural paper and place it where it can easily be seen. ("Because I live, you will live too." [John 14:19b])

Prepare

✓ Write the last section of the Apostles' Creed on a piece of posterboard. You can find the wording at the bottom of this page.

✓ Display the posterboard next to the previous Apostles' Creed posters, where the children will be able to read them.

Creatively Say the Bible Verse

- **Say:** Today's Bible verse is Jesus' promise to his disciples.
- Show the children the Bible verse.
- Invite the children to read the verse with you.
- **Say:** Let's say the verse in a loud voice.
- Encourage the children to read the verse in a loud voice.
- **Say:** Now let's whisper the verse.
- Have the children whisper the verse.
- **Say:** This time let's say the verse slowly.
- Encourage the children to read the verse slowly.
- **Say:** This last time let's read the verse quickly.
- Encourage the children to read the verse quickly.
- **Say:** No matter how you say it, Jesus' promise remains the same.

I Believe in the Resurrection of the Body

- **Say:** The Apostles' Creed helps Christians remember and talk about the things we believe. We have added the last part of the Apostles' Creed to our posters. Today when I ask you "What do you believe?" you will respond by reading the entire Apostles' Creed.
- **Ask:** What do you believe?
- Encourage children to respond by reading the Apostles' Creed.
- Dismiss children to their small groups.

This week's section of the Apostles' Creed:
the resurrection of the body
and the life everlasting. Amen.

Small Groups

Divide the children into small groups. You may organize the groups around age levels or around readers and nonreaders. Keep the groups small, with a maximum of ten children in each group. You may need to have more than one group of each age level.

Young Children

- **Say:** We have been talking a lot about what Christians believe. Let's review what we've talked about. I'm going to read you some statements. If the statement is something Christians believe, show me a thumbs up. If the statement is not something Christians believe, show me a thumbs down.

- Read the following statements to the children and encourage them to respond appropriately.
  o Christians believe in God. (thumbs up)
  o Christians believe you should be mean to people. (thumbs down)
  o Christians believe in Jesus, God's Son. (thumbs up)
  o Christians believe in the Holy Spirit. (thumbs up)
  o Christians believe you should never help people. (thumbs down)
  o Christians believe in the church. (thumbs up)
  o Christians believe in the forgiveness of sins. (thumbs up)
  o Christians believe that love does not exist. (thumbs down)
  o Christians believe in the Resurrection. (thumbs up)

- **Say:** Good job! I can see you know what Christians believe. It's good to know what we believe as Christians. Believing is a choice we make. We choose to follow Jesus.

- Give each child a piece of paper.

- Invite each child to design a poster that says "I believe."

- Encourage the children to decorate their posters.

- **Pray:** God, thank you for your amazing love for us. We choose to believe and to follow Jesus and do your work in the world. Amen.

Prepare
✓ Provide paper and markers.

Prepare

✓ Provide paper and pencils.

Older Children

- **Say:** This is our last week talking about what Christians believe.

- **Ask:** According to the Apostles' Creed, what do Christians believe?

- Allow children an opportunity to review the Christian beliefs discussed in the Apostles' Creed.

- **Say:** The Apostles' Creed was written hundreds of years ago by the early Christians. The creed was used by people who wanted to be baptized in the Christian faith. Before people were baptized, they affirmed what they believed.

- **Ask:** Do you think the Apostles' Creed summarizes everything that is important for Christians to believe? Are there other things that are important for Christians to believe? Are there things in the Apostles' Creed that you think are not necessary for a Christian to believe?

- Allow children an opportunity to share their thoughts. Remind children to respect one another's opinions.

- **Say:** God created us with free will. One thing that means is that we get to choose what we believe. Believing is a choice. Even believing in God is a choice we make. As Christians, we choose to believe certain things as we've discussed during this study. Believing those things affects how we choose to live our lives.

- Give each child a piece of paper and a pencil.

- **Say:** Spend a few moments thinking about what you believe. Then write your own creed. After you have written your creed, you may share it with us if you would like to, but you do not have to. Your creed can be between you and God.

- Allow children time to write.

- Invite any children who wish to do so to share their creeds with the group.

- **Pray:** God, thank you for creating us and loving us. We choose to believe in you and to follow Jesus' example and teachings. Help us to be aware of your Spirit at work within us. We will work together as your church to do your work. Forgive us the ways we have wronged you, just as we also forgive those who have wronged us. Thank you for the good news of the Resurrection and the promise we have in you of eternal life. Amen.

Creed Cards

God	**Church**
Jesus	**Forgiveness**
Holy Spirit	**Resurrection**

Christians Believe in the Resurrection of the Body

Friend 1: Well, this is it. Our last week talking about the Apostles' Creed.

Friend 2: And what Christians believe.

Friend 3: We've learned a lot already. We believe in God. We believe in Jesus.

Friend 4: We believe in the Holy Spirit. We believe in the church.

Friend 5: And we believe in the forgiveness of sins.

Friend 6: What else do Christians believe?

Friend 1: Christians believe in the Resurrection.

Friend 3: That's right! We believe Jesus was raised from the dead.

Friend 5: When Jesus died on the cross, his followers thought that was the end of the story.

Friend 1: What a surprise that first Easter morning when they found the tomb was empty.

Friend 2: Jesus' death was not the end. Jesus is alive!

Friend 6: What about our death? Will we be resurrected?

Friend 3: Jesus promised that because he lived, we would live too.

Friend 4: We don't know exactly what that will be like.

Friend 3: But we know we can trust Jesus' promise.

Friend 2: Let's review what we believe.

Friend 5: We believe in God, the creator of the world.

Friend 6: We believe in Jesus, God's Son.

Friend 4: We believe in the Holy Spirit, God at work within us.

Friend 2: We believe in the church—that all Christians can work together to do God's work.

Friend 5: We believe that God forgives us and we need to forgive others.

Friend 6: We believe in the Resurrection and the promise of eternal life.

Friend 3: Is that everything that Christians believe?

Friend 4: Well, there are lots of other things that Christians believe.

Friend 2: But these are the important things.